Table of Contents

Table of Figures

Introduction

The American government continues to seek a comprehensive, effective communication strategy through which it may project and promote American interests, policies, and objectives abroad. The feeling of some is that the government has been out-communicated since September 11th.[1] A primary cause of this alleged deficiency is likely the failure to recognize that in the contemporary media environment inherent dissimilarities between traditional media and the ubiquitous new media render the utilization of conventional methods and models for strategic communication through the new media an unproductive endeavor.

This paper seeks to illuminate how the new media may be leveraged for the purposes of government and military strategic communication. The characteristics outlined herein are tethered to the overarching idea that audiences *interact* or *engage with*—rather than simply *consume*—the new media. This condition argues for the design of strategic communication efforts conducted via the new media that are conceptualized and planned separately from efforts conducted through traditional media. Government leaders must explicitly recognize and account for fundamental differences between these two distinct media environments—the new and the traditional—as they plan and develop communication strategies.

Definitions

This paper uses the phrase *new media* to describe Internet-based and mobile media that have emerged in roughly the past decade and that continue to evolve today. References and

---

[1] *Strategic Communication Science and Technology Plan*, (Washington, D.C.: Department of Defense Research and Engineering Rapid Reaction Technology Office, April 2009), 2-6; GAO Report to Congressional Committees, *U.S. Public Diplomacy: Key Issues for Congressional Oversight*, May 2009, GAO-09-679SP; Statement of GAO International Affairs and Trade Director Jess T. Ford to U.S. House of Representatives Subcommittee on Science, the Departments of State, Justice, and Commerce, and Related Agencies, *State Department Efforts Lack Certain Communication Elements and Face Persistent Challenges*, May 3, 2006, GAO-06-707T.

allusions to traditional media (radio, television, and print media) are made primarily for comparative purposes. Although much of the focus of this paper will be on the new media, traditional media platforms will continue to hold relevance in any discussion of strategic communication well into the future. Strategic communication conducted through the new media is referred to herein simply as *new media strategic communication.*

A new media *outlet* is distinct from a new media *platform.* In this paper, the former refers to an information channel or communication portal utilized for the purposes of information exchange, whereas the latter refers to the physical conduit through which the information is passed. CNN, *The New York Times*, and NPR are traditional media outlets; Facebook, YouTube, and Twitter are new media outlets. Similarly, television sets, newspapers, and radios are traditional media platforms in the same vein that desktops, laptops, and mobile devices are new media platforms.

This paper borrows an abbreviated definition of strategic communication contained in Joint Publicaton 3-0 (13 February 2008): "focused U.S. Government efforts to understand and engage key audiences to create, strengthen, or preserve conditions favorable for the advancement of U.S. Government interests, policies, and objectives."[2] This paper illustrates how "efforts to understand and engage key audiences" through the new media can only be accomplished through the adoption of dialogic communication practices that treat media as a many-to-many conversation rather than simply a conduit for the one-to-many transmission of messages and information.[3]

---

[2] *Joint Publication 3-0: Joint Operations*, (Washington, D.C.: Department of Defense, February 13, 2008), I-2.
[3] Dialogic communication refers to either a peer-to-peer or many-to-many communication exchange whereby participants seek mutual understanding and, potentially, mutual benefit. This is juxtaposed against a monologic

Although they share many similar characteristics, this paper does not formally address the related functions of public affairs, nor those associated with information operations, psychological operations, covert influence or any other type of information warfare. Strategic communication is treated as one essential form of public diplomacy. Finally, this paper does not utilize the phrase *global engagement*, which is being employed more frequently in official circles. Although the phrase more accurately describes the form of strategic communication depicted herein, *strategic communication* remains more widely used in government and in the popular media.

Literature Review

Government, academia, and even the mass media have produced a considerable body of literature in recent years addressing strategic communication: defining what it is and even what the government should seek to say and how it should say it.[4] However, few writers have sought to distinguish between the new media and traditional media. Communicating through one rather than the other crucially affects how a message will be transmitted, received, interpreted, and in the new media environment, repackaged, repurposed, and retransmitted. Few leaders responsible for funding, designing, and overseeing strategic communication programs have challenged the

---

process whereby a communicator focuses solely on sending but not receiving messages and information. See Robert Perry, "Principles of Strategic Communication for a New Global Commons," (Advanced Research Project, U.S. Naval War College, 6 June 2008), http://www.au.af mil/info-ops/documents/principles_of_sc_naval_wc.pdf (accessed October 15, 2009).

[4] Daniel Matchette, "Marketing as an Element of Strategic Communications" (civilian research project, United States Army War College, April 6, 2006); *U.S. National Strategy for Public Diplomacy and Strategic Communication* (Washington D.C.: National Security Council Policy Coordinating Committee, June 2007); *Principles of Strategic Communication Guide*, (Washington, D.C.: Department of Defense, August 15, 2008); Lawrence Pintak and William A. Rugh, "A New Murrow for US Public Diplomacy," *The Daily Star*, February 17, 2009; William Caldwell, Dennis Murphy, and Anton Menning, "Learning to Leverage New Media," *Military Review*, May-June 2009; Marc Lynch, "The Conversation," *The National*, February 29, 2009; Matt Morgan, "The Rosetta Stone for Strategic Communication? More like Speak 'N Spell," Mountain Runner Blog, entry posted August 31, 2009, http://mountainrunner.us/2009/08/rosetta_or_speaknspell html (accessed January 5, 2010); Carla Mudgett, "Comprehensive U.S. Government Strategic Communication Policy: The Way Forward" (monograph, United States Army Command and General Staff College, School of Advanced Military Studies, 2008-2009).

notion that the nature of new and traditional media is inherently the same. This may result from unfamiliarity with the new media universe. "There are still many people in government—especially higher up in government," writes one group of strategic communication experts, "who have little experience with new communications and information technologies and/or avoid using them."[5]

While many or most government leaders may be on the Internet, few are *in the Internet*, a distinction that will be explained in the last section of this paper that addresses the imminent approach of Web 3.0. In addition, few leaders adequately understand the distinguishing characteristics of the primary new media users involved (widely referred to as "digital natives," or in generational terms, "Millennials") and how they interact with—rather than simply consume—content via the new media. These two key deficiencies have led to normative strategic communication models and methodologies that are incompatible with efforts to design messages that resonate in the new media sphere.

I do not approach this topic as a strategic communication practitioner or expert. Rather, I am an avid new media user and former government new media analyst who has witnessed an array of unsuccessful or only partly successful government attempts to adapt strategic communication efforts to the new media universe. While government efforts have not been wildly successful, neither have most efforts in the private sector. Leveraging the new media for strategic communication is an emerging practice given that the new media universe is itself still evolving. Strategic communicators have more questions than answers with respect to how to effectively engage audiences through the new media. There is no comprehensive model for

---

[5] Steven Corman and Jill Schiefelbein, "Communication and Media Strategy in the Islamist War of Ideas," in *Weapons of Mass Persuasion: Strategic Communication to Combat Violent Extremism,* eds. Steven Corman, Angela Trethewey and H.L. Goodall, Jr. (New York: Peter Lang Publishing, 2008), 86.

strategic communication as it relates *specifically and exclusively* to the new media. In addition, the body of literature addressing new media strategic communication—particularly as it relates to government and the military—as separate and distinct from traditional strategic communication, is still in its infancy. This paper will thus build on a general understanding of strategic communication—that is, one that does not account for the uniqueness and separateness of new media strategic communication—developed by figures such as Colonel William Darley, Dr. Antulio Echevarria, and others within the government and military communities.

Methodology

This paper draws on materials produced by some of the country's preeminent new media minds to highlight the most salient interactive characteristics of the new media—juxtaposed against the passivity of traditional media. The analysis first lays out four principles relevant specifically to military and other government agency strategic communication efforts. Second, this paper applies these principles to the design of new media strategic communication. The thesis that undergirds this examination is that nearly all military and civilian personnel directly involved in kinetic or non-kinetic operations collectively represent the center of gravity for new media strategic communication and must be empowered by military and government leaders to openly and freely communicate strategically in the new media sphere in order for the United State to compete in a rapidly changing and highly complex communication environment.

What is New Media?: Four Principles for Military and Government Strategic Communication

One cannot comprehend the nature of the new media without framing the evolution of the Web, given that the development of the new media is inextricably linked to the Web's evolution.

A useful model for understanding the evolution of the Web and the concurrent progress of the new media universe follows:[6]

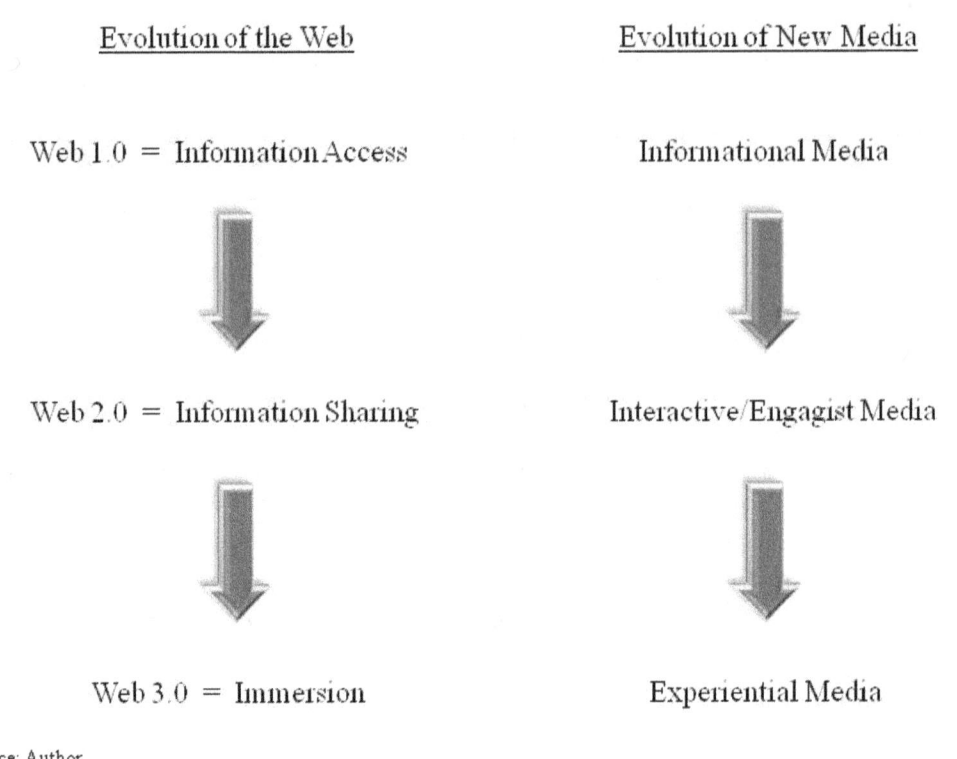

Evolution of the Web Evolution of New Media

Web 1.0 = Information Access Informational Media

Web 2.0 = Information Sharing Interactive/Engagist Media

Web 3.0 = Immersion Experiential Media

Source: Author

Figure 1

Most readers probably understand Web 1.0 quite well. The user experience was characterized by a newfound ability to access an expanding array of information on logically organized portals (think of the Yahoo! or AOL homepage) or to retrieve information using a search engine (think Lycos, Alta Vista, Yahoo!, etc.), all through an appealing graphical user

---

[6] "Evolution of the Web" portion of the graphic adapted from: Susan Wu, "Virtual Worlds and Virtual Humans: NPCs and Avatars" (panel lecture, South by Southwest Interactive Conference, Austin, TX, March 11, 2007).

interface.[7] Web 3.0 and the advent of experiential media are discussed much later. This paper is primarily concerned with Web 2.0—where interactive and engagist media promote information sharing—and its impact on strategic communication.

The new media are social and participatory.

The term Web 2.0 is closely tethered to the notion of social media. Social media are "social" because they are characterized by interaction among (primarily amateur) content producers, exchangers, and/or consumers. In fact, many consumers of social media are also producers of social media. For instance, if you watch video posted to a friend's Facebook profile page, but also upload and/or embed original video on your own profile page, you are both a consumer and a producer of social media. In industry parlance, you would be described as a *prosumer*. Although not directly addressed in this paper, it is important to note that media ecology is an entire field devoted to examining how interaction among actors (e.g. prosumers) within a complex communication environment (as well as between actors and new media technology) affects the meaning of messages.

The new media are inherently social and their social characteristics—most importantly that of interaction—help us to understand the participatory nature of the new media universe. The new media facilitate participation in that "the means of production are widely available and content creation is not based on traditional editorial structures."[8] Below is a graphical illustration of the contemporary new media universe; this universe will undoubtedly be very different in a few years as it continues to expand and evolve.

---

[7] For simplicity's sake, in describing Web 1.0 I do not include the nature of the World Wide Web prior to the arrival of the graphical user interface.
[8] Ivan Sigal, *Digital Media in Conflict-Prone Societies*, (Washington, DC: Center for International Media Assistance, 19 October, 2009), 10.

The New Media Universe

DUE TO COPYRIGHT RESTRICTIONS
SOME OR ALL IMAGES ARE NOT INCLUDED

Figure 2

One of the first efforts to document the power of participation and the ability of a particular group to leverage social media for strategic communication purposes was the 1998 book entitled *The Zapatista Social Netwar in Mexico*. The Zapatista movement was novel in that it established what was perhaps the world's first global "informational guerilla movement"[9] and set the precedent for what authors Thomas Rid and Marc Hecker would later conceive of as a

---

[9] John Arquilla, David Ronfeldt, Graham Fuller, and Melissa Fuller, *The Zapatista Social Netwar in Mexico* (Washington, DC: RAND Publishing, 1998), 117.

"social form" of warfare conducted largely through social media.[10] Through e-mail distribution lists, message boards, and discussion forums, a small cadre of Zapatistas and their sympathizers "engaged activists from far and wide" and were able to rally "a multitude of foreign activists...to swarm—electronically and physically—out of the United States, Canada, and Europe into Mexico City and Chiapas"[11] The broad and swift dissemination of Zapatista propaganda was unprecedented for a non-state actor and brought significant international attention to the situation, forcing Mexico's government to address the Zapatista issue with extreme prudence. The Mexican foreign minister at the time referred to the rebellion as simply "a war on the Internet."[12]

As a student working toward a degree in Latin American Studies in Austin, Texas—a hotbed for Zapatista activism in the United States—at the time of the rebellion, I witnessed how the Zapatistas and their sympathizers utilized early forms of social media to engage a global audience and co-opt the direct or indirect participation of thousands of prosumers in their struggle. By communicating strategically through social media, the Zapatistas succeeded in their efforts to "shape beliefs and attitudes in the surrounding social milieu," as a growing number of students and local activists in Austin and numerous other cities in the Western world began mobilizing to bring direct international political pressure to bear on the Mexican government to meet some or all of the Zapatista's demands.[13] These activists were also instrumental in transferring clothing, food, and money to the Zapatistas prior to the Mexican government's restrictions on travel in and out of the affected region.

---

[10] See Thomas Rid and Marc Hecker, *War 2.0: Irregular Warfare in the Information Age* (Westport, CT: Praeger International, 2009).
[11] Arquilla, *Zapatista Social Netwar*, xi, 3.
[12] Ibid., 4.
[13] Ibid., 21.

The new media represent a many-to-many conversation.

The Zapatistas did not—perhaps could not—rely on traditional print and broadcast media to convey their view of the situation to the outside world. Instead, they adopted a many-to-many communication model that involved networks of sympathizers—first in the Chiapas region, then Mexico as a whole, and eventually throughout the world—exchanging messages and information via electronic distribution lists, message boards, and discussion forums. Tapping into and growing these networks as quickly as the Zapatistas did would not have been possible without the effective utilization of early social media platforms. Corporate and government media were almost entirely circumvented, as the communication networks expanded organically from a local base outward through networks that spanned the globe.

The Zapatista case study encapsulates many of the social characteristics of the new media. It also illustrates a rudimentary form of citizen participation in the media sphere. In the intervening years as the new media have continued to evolve, new forms of amateur involvement and participation in the media sphere have appeared. Blogs, video blogs (vlogs), mobile blogs (moblogs), video sharing services (YouTube, DailyMotion), lifecasting platforms (Justin.tv, Ustream) and other user-generated content services that encourage, and in some cases require, reader or viewer feedback and/or interaction among prosumers have transformed the nature of media (the new media, at least) into a many-to-many conversation. As one author states, "for the first time in human history, our communication tools support the group conversation and group action."[14]

---

[14] Clay Shirky, *Here Comes Everybody*, (New York: Penguin Press, 2008), front book flap.

The new media are immediate, readily accessible, and indifferent to the distinction between strategic and operational communication.

In 1999, the WTO Ministerial Conference in Seattle collapsed amid a chaotic scene of large-scale anti-globalization protests that severely hampered—and at times paralyzed—movement by conference participants in the downtown area. Disparate networks of groups opposed to globalization (labor unions, student groups, environmentalists, religious bodies, anarchists, etc.) organized intra- and inter-group action through Web-based and mobile new media prior to and during the protests. The "Battle in Seattle," as these wholly effective protests came to be known, represented the first time that emerging media platforms and tools had been employed on a massive scale to communicate and coordinate direct action in real time.

Similarly, in 2001, Joseph Estrada was ousted as the Philippines president during what was dubbed, "The Pager Revolution," as disaffected citizens began exchanging the simple text message: "Go to EDSA"—a reference to the famous shrine on Manila's main thoroughfare, Epifania de los Santos Avenue. The use of mobile group messaging tactics (also referred to as "text mobbing") by anti-Estrada Filipinos was critical in amassing what was initially a small but vocal crowd around the shrine the evening before Estrada was ousted. As news of the scene spread overnight by word-of-mouth as well as text message, more people began streaming toward the EDSA shrine. By 6:00am the next morning, 700,000 raucous demonstrators had collected. Reading the writing on the wall, the military withdrew its support of Estrada that morning and he was forced to step down. [15]

---

[15] Sandra Burton, "People Power Redux," *Time Asia*, January 29, 2001, http://www.time.com/time/asia/magazine/2001/0129/cover1.html, (accessed December 2, 2009).

Since 2001, new media observers have witnessed groups make use of other new media tools and platforms to effect change, albeit typically on a much smaller scale. It was not until 2008 that the world again witnessed mobilization through new media platforms and tools on a massive scale. Early in 2008, peace activists coordinated an event called One Million Voices Against the FARC entirely through the Facebook social networking website. The event brought over one million demonstrators into the streets in 192 cities and 39 countries to protest drug-related violence by the FARC. [16] In 2009, Moldova experienced what is termed a "Twitter Revolution" after demonstrators organized in real time via the Twitter microblogging service to violently protest the Communist Party's alleged fraudulent claim of victory in April 2009 elections.[17] In Iran, as was widely documented by traditional mainstream media outlets, Twitter and Facebook were instrumental during the summer of 2009 in the organization and growth of demonstrations against voting irregularities and government violence following the reelection of President Ahmedinejad.

What each of these events underscores is that the space-time continuum for communication has collapsed, and with it has gone the distinction between communication as a strategic imperative and communication as an operational enabler. The exchange of information during the Moldovan and Iranian protests could be monitored and/or acted upon locally and from afar, literally in real time, through Twitter and Twitter aggregators such as Twazzup, and in near real-time through social networking websites like Facebook and Odnoklassniki.ru and citizen media initiatives like tehranlive.org.

---

[16] "New Media Enables Worldwide March Against FARC," report FEA20080206526707 (accessed November 15, 2009), and "Millions Paralyzed Country Marching Against FARC," Caracol Radio, February 4, 2008, report LAP20080204070001(accessed November 15, 2009), both reports accessible at https://www.opensource.gov.
[17] "Moldova's 'Twitter Revolutionary' Speaks Out" *BBC News Online*, April 25, 2009, report EUP20090427167002 (accessed November 15, 2009), accessible at https://www.opensource.gov.

The convergence of strategic and operational communication will force leaders to think of "strategic" communication conducted not just as discrete "campaigns" conducted over weeks, months, or years, but also as a continuous real-time operation or series of operations. That is, organizations can make use of the same new media platforms and outlets for both strategic purposes (to win hearts and minds over time) and for operational purposes (to organize, coordinate, mobilize, monitor and/or in some other fashion act out). The important distinction is that groups and organizations cannot use traditional media for both purposes, because information is not exchanged through traditional media with the same immediacy (to the extent that information is exchanged at all rather than simply broadcast outward) and because most non-state actors and individuals are barred from making frequent use of traditional (corporate) media to disseminate messages and information. The problems of lag time and access itself point to the fact that traditional media may be used for conducting traditional *strategic* communication, whereas the new media are helping transform "strategic" communication into a unitary *strategic and operational* system of information exchange that can be employed for both long-term strategic and shorter term operational purposes. This idea will be revisited later during the discussion of Web 3.0.

In the new media sphere, coordination trumps planning.

The pervasiveness of the new media means that users increasingly have immediate access *to* their communication network and thus *with* their social network(s). But a social network is a term that should be understood in very general terms in the new media sphere. Social networks are typically thought of as semi-static and semi-permanent. That is, most of us do not gain or lose members of our social network every day or even every week. Our social network in the new media sphere is largely a reflection of our network of friends, acquaintances and co-workers in the real world. But the pervasiveness and immediacy of the new media also allow for unique forms of impermanent social networks, such as the flash mob. The flash mob was originally designed as a gathering of complete strangers, organized via the Web and mobile devices, who quickly organized to perform a pointless act and then immediately dispersed. The first flash mob was convened as part of an innocuous social experiment in 2003 by a New York journalist.[18] Since then (mostly) young adults and teenagers have experimented with the flash mob phenomenon in nearly every corner of the globe. Somewhere along the line, however, we began observing not-so-innocuous emergent characteristics of flash mobs that spontaneously congregated in a defined geographic space. One of the first instances of a nefarious flash mob was in Dublin, Ireland in February 2006.[19]

The flash mob is a variation of the more generic *smart mob*, a term coined by Howard Rheingold in his groundbreaking 2002 book by the same name.[20] The distinguishing characteristic of a flash mob is that its intent or purpose is not typically defined very long before the group converges for action—if the intent is defined prior to the event at all—whereas a more generic smart mob usually conceives of and/or coordinates its intent or purpose via the new media days, weeks, or even months before action takes place. The means of communication are the same, but the aggregation of participants is not necessarily spontaneous as it is with a flash mob. In both cases, coordination also occurs in real time while the act is taking place, meaning that emergent behavior is possible or even probable in both instances. Importantly, behavior emerging from real-time coordination through new media platforms and outlets can render

---

[18] Bill Wasik, "My Crowd, Or, Phase 5: A Report From the Inventor of the Flash Mob," *Harper's Magazine*, March 2006, 56-66.
[19] Chekov Feeney, Vincent Browne, John Byrne and Colm Heatley, "Flames of Rage: How the Riots Happened and Why," *Village*, March 2006.
[20] Howard Rheingold, *Smart Mobs: The Next Social Revolution* (New York: Perseus Books, 2002).

advance operational planning moot, or at very least argues for distributed continuous adaptive planning in near real-time by those acting in a given operational environment.

How does an understanding of new media inform the design of strategic communication?

Having identified four fundamental characteristics of the new media as they relate to strategic communication, this paper now turns to a more substantive discussion of how the new media should inform the design of more effective communication strategies.

New media strategic communication attempts to influence, not control, the conversation.

Strategic communicators, in reality, never controlled the messages they sent into the media universe. Print and broadcast media outlets and other "mediators" have always interpreted and re-framed messages for media consumers. Communication models that identified message senders and message receivers as the sole action agents involved in communication were invalid in the traditional media universe of 1950 as much as they are in the contemporary new media universe.

Through the new media communicators now have a direct line of sight with their audience, namely media prosumers. Ironically, however, the removal of the message gatekeeper has only made strategic communication more complex, as there are now an even greater number of credible interlocutors within a prosumer's social network that shape and influence how and within what context an individual decodes and interprets a message.

To reiterate, the paradigm of the American government as message sender and *The New York Times* or CNN as mediator or gatekeeper applies only to the traditional media sphere. In the new media universe, communicators engage directly with message receivers who are in their own right message senders. These prosumers reuse, repackage, and repurpose the information a communicator has conveyed to them for their own message-sending activities. The message originator cannot control what or how the modified message is exchanged among prosumers at an organic level. The originator may only purposefully attempt to control an initial message input(s), and thereby influence *thematically* the course of a discrete media conversation.

A discrete media conversation taking place within a complex communication environment will continually evolve, be subsumed by or converge with other discrete media conversations, and will, overall, take on a life of its own; a life that the message originator cannot predict. That is, questions, conclusions, actions, behaviors, and other activities by and among participants in the new media universe will emerge during the flow of the conversation that extend well beyond the intent of the originator's initial message input.

And herein lies perhaps the biggest problem with military and government leaders who still view press conferences and press releases as the primary means with which to convey a message to either a general or target audience. *The act of conveying a message through a press conference or press release is an incomplete action.* If an initial message-sending activity altogether neglects the follow-on conversation that takes place in the new media sphere once the press conference has concluded or the press release has been widely disseminated, the activity has failed from a new media standpoint.

To say another way, press conferences, press releases, blog entries, and Facebook posts as discrete acts that do not account for the message as it moves and evolves in the new media universe are of limited value. A press conference, press release, blog entry, Facebook post, etc. represents a single message input. If further inputs or contributions are not made as the message evolves within a larger media conversation, then the efficacy of the communication activity has been compromised, and there is little chance that the objectives associated with a strategic communication effort will be realized.

An official press conference may last thirty minutes. The intended message or messages are conveyed to mediators (correspondents from, say, Al-Jazirah or ABC News) who will package the message(s) into a 5 to 10-second sound bite and impart meaning ("spin") as they convey the message(s) to media consumers. That 5 to 10-second segment is all that the vast majority of media consumers will know of the original message(s) communicated by American officials at the press conference.

But in the new media sphere, prosumers will repackage and repurpose the original message(s) conveyed at the press conference (and the message as spun by disparate traditional media), and the conversation on a specific topic will continue. If the message originator (e.g. the Defense Department) does not participate in the conversation taking place in the new media sphere, then the message originator has surrendered the ability to influence the media conversation, let alone to attempt to control it. A press conference, press release, blog entry, or Facebook post is a first act; a necessary but insufficient undertaking in support of strategic communication objectives.

Participating in any media conversation can be a time-consuming activity. Participating in multiple conversations simultaneously can present a severe resource drain. In practical terms, a press conference, press release, blog entry, or Facebook post that serves as the initial and the final (that is, the only) undertaking in a strategic communication activity is much easier than maintaining multiple conversations in the new media sphere. But while traditional one-way, monologic communication methods may be easier in both conceptual and practical terms, it is also woefully less effective. As one communication scholar submits, "If the U.S. government's strategic goal is to win the hearts and minds of diverse others, the most effective form of communication is dialogue, not monologue."[21]

Apart from the time and personnel drain that some believe dialogue through the new media will entail, another argument against new media strategic communication relates to the loss of message control: the new media permit the corruption of messages as they were intended to be decoded and interpreted. Thus, the conundrum emerges that if organizations do not engage through the new media they will lose relevancy and slide into an uncomfortable oblivion in the new media sphere; if leaders do encourage engagement through the new media, their organizations will lose much of their institutional authority, power, and control.[22]

Yet, as argued previously, message control has largely been a chimera and messages conveyed by government agencies have never been as internally consistent and universally effective as many leaders believe. Nor have audiences considered the American government to be particularly authoritative or truthful since the emergence of the "credibility gap" half a century ago, if not before then. Furthermore, no military or civilian leader should assume that any message intended for a foreign audience will ever be received without a healthy dose of skepticism.

In new media strategic communication credibility is more important than authority and message context is as important as message content.

If information disseminated by the American government is perceived both domestically and, especially, abroad to be less ingenuous than many leaders realize or admit, how might

---

[21] H.L. Goodall, Jr., Amgela Trethewey and Kelly McDonald, "Strategic Ambiguity, Communication, and Public Diplomacy in an Uncertain World," in *Weapons of Mass Persuasion: Strategic Communication to Combat Violent Extremism,* eds. Steven Corman, Angela Trethewey and H.L. Goodall, Jr. (New York: Peter Lang Publishing, 2008), 31.
[22] David Weinberger, *Everything is Miscellaneous: The Power of the New Global Disorder* (New York: Times Books, 2007), 33.

organizations establish standing in the new media sphere and thus retain the capacity to influence behavior? The most popular answer to this question is that government actions takes must mesh with rhetoric. In simpler terms, the government is often seen as saying one thing and doing another. The lofty idealism of American strategic communication fails to match the messy realism of events on the ground. Official strategic communication efforts are often seen as duplicitous attempts to misrepresent the true nature of an issue or event.

In reality, deliberate duplicity rarely comes into play in the realm of strategic communication. Rather, in hierarchical structures information travels down the hierarchy more efficiently than up or laterally because of the inability of those at the top of the hierarchy to properly filter out extraneous and multifarious information flows while at the same time retaining that which is critically pertinent. That is, leaders and strategic communicators may communicate strategically without having an accurate picture of the true nature of a situation when information about that situation must travel up or horizontally within an organizational or inter-organizational hierarchy. This is not to suggest that strategic or operational considerations—or politics for that matter—never impinge upon what will and will not be said during a strategic communication activity, only that there is rarely, if ever, an intent to purposefully misinform through strategic communication. Put another way, disinformation is not the currency of strategic communication.

Before the advent of new media, "authority" mattered. In the traditional one-to-many communication environment, the notion of a unitary authoritative actor (a government agency, for instance) conveying information to the masses held some relevance in so far as objective gatekeepers (traditional media) were able to faithfully re-present the message to media consumers. In the new media sphere, a unitary authority is less commonly accepted or recognized by a wide swath of prosumers. A government agency is one actor among many with a message input. Authority is, therefore, less germane to the discussion of new media strategic communication than the notion of credibility.

Authority was largely conferred automatically upon established unitary actors in the traditional media sphere, whereas credibility and its effect on message meaning and clarity in the new media sphere is something that resides within the context of one's social networks where personal relationships are firmly established and trust continually nurtured. As one group of researchers submits, "message clarity and perception of meaning is a function of relationships, not strictly of word usage."[23] More succinctly put, "meanings are in social networks, not in words."[24] The credibility of an actor in the new media communication environment is crucial to how a message is decoded and interpreted by other actors. Because an actor's credibility is both relative and not absolute—which suggests that an actor may be very credible to one individual and slightly or significantly less so to another—any message inputted into the new media sphere and replicated through disparate social networks has an inestimable number of meanings depending not on the intent of the message originator but by virtue of how and where the message is exchanged among networked prosumers.

Herein lies the importance of recognizing that the new media represent a conversation. By waging discrete strategic communication "campaigns" designed to influence perceptions of a specific issue or situation, communicators are disengaged or insulated from the ongoing flow of

---

[23] Goodall, Trethewey and McDonald, "Strategic Ambiguity," 28.
[24] Steven Corman, Angela Trethewey, and H.L. Goodall, Jr., "Creating a New Communication Policy: How Changing Assumptions Leads to New Strategic Objectives," in *Weapons of Mass Persuasion: Strategic Communication to Combat Violent Extremism,* eds. Steven Corman, Angela Trethewey and H.L. Goodall, Jr. (New York: Peter Lang Publishing, 2008), 183.

the conversation. Effective new media strategic communicators cannot construct messages outside the context of a specific media conversation because messages in the new media sphere are, as one scholar reasons, "never disconnected from the ongoing narrative stream that informs, surrounds, and constitutes them."[25] Message origination and subsequent inputs or contributions to the conversation must be made continuously from within the conversation or narrative stream. Strategic communication campaigns instigated and conducted from without the narrative stream results in a disjointed and unproductive strategic communication effort. This paper will revisit the topic of strategic communication "campaigns" in greater detail later.

The meta-message is as important as the core message.

The potency and marketability of a message does not depend solely on the content of the core message, but also on its meta-message. The meta-message is the "vibe" extending beyond (meta) the core message and can refer to:

- the outlet chosen to deliver the message (Facebook, YouTube, a video blog, mobile blog, a virtual world or game environment, etc.).

- the individual, group, or other entity exchanging or sharing the message (someone in my Facebook social network, an organization I follow on Twitter, an unsolicited SMS, etc.).

- the platform through which the message is delivered (mobile device, the Web, Xbox, etc.).

- the personality or actor delivering the message, if applicable.

---

[25] Steven Corman, Angela Trethewey, and H.L. Goodall, Jr., "Strategery: Missed Opportunities and the Consequences of Obsolete Strategic Communication Theory," in *Weapons of Mass Persuasion: Strategic Communication to Combat Violent Extremism,* eds. Steven Corman, Angela Trethewey and H.L. Goodall, Jr. (New York: Peter Lang Publishing, 2008), 6.

- a video or audio message's production value, to include the colors and graphics used in a visual message.

The meta-message is the atmospherics surrounding the core message. In truth, many of these meta-message components are important to communication through traditional media as well, but the interactive nature of the new media and the proliferation of new media outlets have given rise to more nuances of meta-messages and made the concept even more important to grasp when communicating strategically through the new media.

A core message in its naked form may not resonate with an intended demographic. However, when coupled with its meta-message, that core message takes on new significance. Even if a core message is not initially compelling, its meta-message may make it palatable to a specific demographic or audience segment. I may not believe that the American effort in Afghanistan is futile or unjust, but if several of my friends on the Hi5 social networking website think so and exchange slick media to that effect, I may become more accepting of (or susceptible to) that message. A hypothetical 16 year-old in Paris or Madrid may not seek out extremist propaganda on the Internet, but may over time become more accepting of it after watching subtitled jihadist videos embedded on her classmate's Netlog profile page, or raw videos of American contractors shooting at Iraqi civilians on LiveLeak.com. Neither I nor the 16 year-old may agree with the core message being conveyed, but it is the meta-message that makes it palatable and potentially potent.

Transnational jihadist movements understand that the marketing of a *global* ideology depends on reaching (primarily young) demographic groups throughout the world and mobilizing a diverse network of both hardcore adherents and jihadist sympathizers. Messages may be made available through new media outlets popular in the West and tailored to Western Muslims through the use of video featuring native English (or French, or Spanish, etc.) speakers, charismatic orators, subtitles, voice-overs, special effects, video mashups,[26] etc., while also marketing their propaganda to niche audience segments in other corners of the globe using culturally relevant meta-messages.

As *A Globe and Mail* article submits:

> This is the new jihad – the evolution of a propaganda effort that, just a decade ago, consisted mostly of Osama bin Laden speeches on video tapes smuggled out of a hideout in Afghanistan. Today, the public-relations arms of terrorist organizations – run less by grizzled warriors than by 20-something computer geeks – deal in digital currency, getting their messages out instantly and universally using the scope and anonymity of the web.
>
> The process is borderless. A beheading video moves from a hideout in Peshawar to a server in London to a computer screen in Toronto unhindered…
>
> All manner of video, audio and even interactive propaganda have found an audience among many disaffected Muslim youth around the world. But while the majority of people who download such content may only fuel a passive resentment of the West, for others the audiovisual diatribes of Mr. bin Laden and his kin have served as a sort of gateway drug to a more violent worldview.[27]

The challenge for government communicators is to engage prosumers in the new media universe with niche audience and context-specific messages that reflect conscious attention to the intrinsic meta-message. Two fascinating and easy-to-understand methodologies that drive to the heart of how strategic communicators (and others) can implement different techniques to create meta-messages more apt to help a core message influence and persuade specific audience segments—as well as how to explicate meta-messages in an adversary's messages—are the

---

[26] A video mashup consists of elements from two or more pre-existing videos combined to make a new video.
[27] Omar El Akkad, "Terror Goes Digital," *The Globe and Mail*, 3 April 2009, http://www.theglobeandmail.com/news/national/article777472.ece.

Visual Persuasion Methodology and *Audience Resonance Methodology* available to all government and military personnel.[28]

"Command and facilitate" versus "command and control."

If the new media are a conversation then hierarchical control is a problem in the Web 2.0 universe of new media strategic communication, because, as David Bohm has said, "hierarchy is antithetical to dialogue."[29] Actually, hierarchy was a problem in Web 1.0 as well, if control by a mediating entity limited access to information (hence AOL, once the most popular "walled garden" online community, was forced to transform itself from a self-contained universe of information disconnected from the larger World Wide Web into a normal Web portal, or otherwise face extinction). Much of Web 2.0 is based on the non-hierarchical editorial control of information, hence the popularity of social news websites like Digg and Reddit[30] (to which nearly all traditional media outlets with a presence on the Web now encourage users to post/share the outlet's copyrighted content directly from the outlet's own website). This also helps explain the popularity of social video sharing websites like YouTube and the Arab world's Ikbis, and social networking websites like Facebook and South Korea's Cyworld.

In military operations, control is an instrument of command. However, as David Alberts and Richard Hayes submit in their widely-cited book *Power to the Edge*, because control reduces flexibility "control comes at a price."[31] This paper seeks to elucidate the idea that the immediacy

---

[28] To download hardcopies of these methodologies see product numbers FEA20080514675827 and FEA20090717871401 at www.opensource.gov.

[29] David Bohm cited in Peter Senge, *The Fifth Discipline: The Art and Practice of the Learning Organization* (New York: Doubleday, 2006), 228.

[30] Digg and Reddit are social news websites where prosumers submit, comment on, and vote on the merit or value of specific news items.

[31] David Alberts and Richard Hayes, *Power to the Edge: Command and Control in the Information Age* (Washington, DC: CCRP Publications, 2003), 18.

of the new media renders strategic communicators' flexibility to exchange information in real or near real time of paramount importance if they are to successfully engage audiences. Command and control (C2) approaches that involve the issuance of highly detailed directives from higher command to subordinates are not conducive to new media strategic communication. In fact, any control mechanism that closely regulates or restricts specific tasks or operations is a disabler in the conduct of new media strategic communication. While control helps mitigate risk, it most often also retards the free flow of information. In so doing, it impedes proper functioning of feedback mechanisms in the new media sphere and reduces the overall efficacy of new media strategic communication, given that the new media conversation evolves organically and in real time. Warfare is by nature non-linear, and as Marine Corps doctrine argues, commanders should seek only to "impose a general framework of order" and not attempt to exercise "precise, positive control" when operating in a complex environment.[32] With respect to the complex task of communicating effectively through the new media—where platforms change by the month and actors exploiting these platforms interact in real time—control mechanisms take you out of the conversation. What instrument, then, must functional command utilize in broadly overseeing new media strategic communication? This is a question private sector firms continue to grapple with, as well.

Alberts and Hayes describe a "control free" approach to C2 as one in which commanders are focused only on "creating *initial* conditions that maximize the likelihood of mission accomplishment [emphasis added]," as well as the "resources necessary for the force elements to succeed."[33] Higher command does not seek to maintain exclusive control over an operation or

---

[32] Marine Corps, *Field Manual 1: Warfighting* (Washington, DC: Department of the Navy, 1989), 9.

[33] Alberts and Hayes, *Power to the Edge*, 25.

function. In the context of new media strategic communication, a focus on initial conditions would necessarily involve the provision of information technologies and tools (new media platforms) as well as a relaxation of regulations that inhibit persistent access to the new media marketplace where information is exchanged. From that point forward, higher command's role would be largely undetectable.

Such an approach is not, in actual fact, a form of command and control, but, rather, a method of *facilitating* new media strategic communication's role in the achievement of broad national or military objectives and the overall long-term mission. Facilitating rather than controlling is the essential role of commanders *in* the information battlefield. Through a facilitation mindset, higher command, in essence, flattens the hierarchical oversight of new media strategic communication. In so doing, they reduce friction and bureaucratic inertia, and allow communicators to innovate, adapt, and coordinate their efforts continually, instantaneously and organically.

Semi-autonomous, self-synchronized, and operationally embedded cells represent one alternative for new media strategic communication.

While hierarchy obviously should not be purged entirely in the execution of new media strategic communication functions, these functions are better effected by small, self-synchronized (meaning largely autonomous) cells of communicators assigned to work against a specific issue or group. The successful operation of such cells requires competent strategic communicators that understand the nature of the broader mission, share a common situational awareness, and that are fully integrated, meaning that there is a high degree of trust among cell members, as well as between cell members and the facilitating commander.[34]

The relationship between cell collectives and functional command enumerated above is not unlike the "distributed control with central command" scenario described in Marine doctrine,[35] or the concept of "hybridization" that one author expresses as the attempt to "harness the flexibility and adaptability of networks while preserving some hierarchical features."[36] While it does not go as far, this relationship also represents one (not insignificant) step toward former Air Force officer John Robb's argument for a complete decentralization of both command and control in government and military communication practices in the fight against our highly networked terrorist adversaries.[37]

While the hierarchical aspect of these hybrid entities is not unfamiliar to Defense Department leaders, the complete downward delegation of control may be a difficult idea to embrace for some, given the perceived greater opportunity for error and the unanticipated consequences that this breed of strategic communication will engender. However, as demonstrated quantitatively in the non-linear sciences and evidenced in the qualitative study of hybrid organizations such as the aforementioned Zapatistas, "decentralized systems of quasi-autonomous units can operate more effectively and with a greater degree of adaptability on the basis of the local calculations of the networked agents constituting them."[38] Said another way,

---

[34] Arthur K. Cebrowski and John J. Garstka, "Network-Centric Warfare: Its Origins and Future," *U.S. Naval Institute Proceedings Magazine,* January 1998, 28-35.

[35] Yaneer Bar-Yam, *Making Things Work: Solving Complex Problems in a Complex World* (Brookline, MA: Knowledge Press, 2004), 110.

[36] Antoine Bousquet, *The Scientific Way of Warfare: Order and Chaos on the Battlefields of Modernity* (New York: Columbia University Press, 2009), 210.

[37] See John Robb, *Brave New War: The Next Stage of Terrorism and the End of Globalization,*" (Hoboken, NJ: John Wiley & Sons, 2007).

[38] Bousquet, *The Scientific Way of Warfare,* 182.

"parts operate as independent systems with the ability to be relatively self-controlling and yet act as responsible members of a coherent system with the ability to respond effectively to the requirements of their containing whole."[39] Serious but infrequent errors by semi-autonomous cell collectives during the conduct of this brand of strategic communication will certainly occur, but the aggregate long-term benefits of distributed control in terms of immediacy, credibility, and efficacy of the message (that is, the contribution to the conversation) far outweigh the perceived benefits of continuing the risk-averse strategy of vetting and scrutinizing from on high official and "authoritative" government messages.

In new media strategic communication, messages and information do not flow from the self-synchronized cell to large mediators (Al-Jazirah, *Le Monde*, BBC Radio, etc.) that interpret and relay messages to the masses. Instead, individual communicators will spend much of their time communicating through citizen or social media outlets with individuals who represent only themselves (that is, they are unaffiliated or independent actors) or a small group, rather than a large, homogenous organization. In lieu of, or in addition to, making available or disseminating information to representatives of print or broadcast media outlets in the hope that they use the information as intended and forward (that is, broadcast) this information on to media consumers, information may be exchanged directly with prosumers through the new media.

There indeed exist nascent efforts in the military and government to communicate through social media, but the two most publicized approaches merit close examination. First, the State Department's Digital Outreach Team engages foreign audiences through a practice known as "comment blogging." In a nutshell, the Digital Outreach Team combs through the comment

---

[39] Jamshid Gharajedaghi, *Systems Thinking: Managing Chaos and Complexity* (Boston: Elsevier Publishing, 2006), 317.

sections of prominent foreign blogs (primarily Arabic and Farsi-language blogs). When an issue involving the United States or its interests is identified, an individual on the team, when appropriate, publishes a comment to encapsulate or clarify the official American position. Other readers will often respond to the comment, prompting further comment by the Digital Outreach Team, the blogger himself/herself, and/or other prosumers. In this manner, the Digital Outreach Team is participating in one facet of the media conversation, although it should be noted that each comment is vetted from above prior to its posting. The State Department has continued to display risk-averse behavior by retaining both command *and* control at a higher level, thereby hindering the emergence of a prototype self-synchronized cell to build upon.

The Defense Department's Digital Engagement Team has a slightly wider purview. It has been involved with the launch of an array of social media communication projects. Initiatives thus far have included microblogging efforts (Twitter), and the creation of Facebook fan pages, YouTube channels, and Flickr photostreams, to name but a few. These efforts represent a significant step in the right direction, however many—but certainly not all—of these platforms are simply being used to broadcast information out, while largely neglecting the intake of feedback and responses from prosumers. Obviously, the resources needed to do so are beyond the scope of the Digital Engagement Team, and the objective of a given initiative is not always to seek dialogue, particularly when the audience already maintains a positive disposition toward the services, as is the case, for example, with U.S. Central Command's Facebook page.[40] However, if Defense Department strategic communication as a component of a broader global engagement strategy seeks to engage and retain the attention of foreign audiences in particular, the Defense Department must divest itself of its traditional "heavy reliance on an antiquated, linear, and

---

[40] This judgment is based on the fact that the vast majority of Central Command's Facebook "fans" are American and post comments on the page that reflect a favorable attitude toward the military services.

simplistic influence model of communication"[41] and begin to employ an authentically dialogic model of communication.

New media strategic communication actively seeks feedback.

The purpose of this paper is not to evaluate the merits or demerits of specific communication models and recommend that the government form its communication strategy around one model as opposed to any other. Instead, this paper highlights some of the intrinsic differences between traditional and new media, arguing that any model that fails to treat communication through the new media in isolation from communication through traditional media is problematic. This paper has posited that the new media universe as a system of communication among diverse, interacting agents is interactive and kinetic, while the traditional media universe is grounded in linear, one-to-many communication between agents, and is decidedly more passive.

The separateness of strategic communication in the new media and traditional media spheres is nowhere more pronounced than in the examination of the role of feedback. Others have adequately evaluated the merits and demerits of specific communication models as they relate to government strategic communication, concluding that the Pragmatic Complexity Model of communication is most appropriate for contemporary strategic communication efforts.[42] The Pragmatic Complexity Model is a communication model grounded in complexity science, thus the model maintains that feedback among agents is a central feature of a complex system of communication. The importance of feedback in the Pragmatic Complexity Model also calls

---

[41] Corman, Trethewey, and Goodall, "Creating a New Communication Policy," 4.
[42] See Mark B. Sherkey, "Strong Horses—Systems Thinking—Strategic Communication" (monograph, United States Army Command and General Staff College, School of Advanced Military Studies, 2008-2009).

attention to the fact that feedback mechanisms in many traditional communication models are wholly absent. This points not just to the inadequacy of said models for contemporary strategic communication but, more fundamentally, to the complete absence of feedback mechanisms in the traditional media universe itself. It is not simply the models that are no longer universally valid; given their inability to generate feedback, the traditional media themselves are wholly deficient in the conduct of new media strategic communication.

The flow of messages and information in the traditional media universe followed a linear, one-to-many pattern among agents and is represented—somewhat simplistically—in the graphic below.

Information Flow in the Traditional Media Universe

Information Sender

Traditional Media

Media Consumers

Source: Author

Figure 3

31

In contrast, the new media have not only made feedback much easier, but in some cases a requisite for participation in the media conversation. Additionally, the number of interacting agents within the new media sphere is much greater, as represented below, although the actual number of agents and scale of interaction is only broadly depicted.

Information Flow in the Contemporary Media Universe

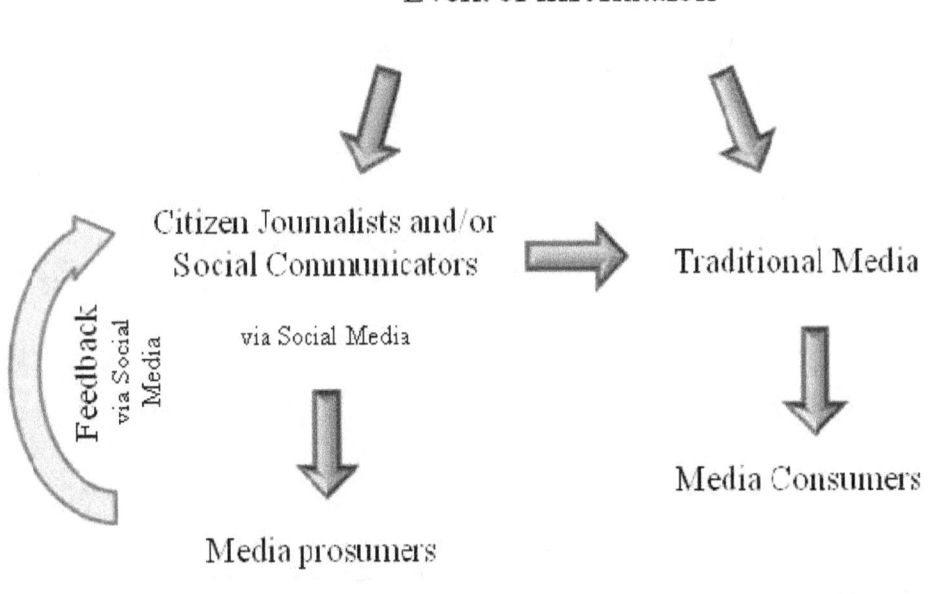

Source: Author

Figure 4

NYU communication professor Douglas Rushkoff writes that effective communicators today utilize the new media to generate feedback, arguing that "from phones to blogs to podcasts—we have gained the capacity to generate feedback, and as a result our ideas are

32

exchanged more organically, rapidly, unpredictably, and—most important—uncontrollably than ever before."[43]

By contrast, strategic communication efforts tethered to traditional models do not allow feedback from message recipients or media consumers. Rushkoff goes so far as to portray terrorist propaganda as a "contagious set of destructive commands" representing uncontrolled feedback by highly networked agents within a complex social system. The proliferation of terrorist propaganda is due in no small part to "the lack of constructive conversation—about the West's relationship with Islam, our own Arab citizens, and the human suffering we might permit in the Middle East to feed our oil addiction—that remains charged beneath the surface, waiting for detonation."[44]

To be proactive in acting against terrorist propaganda, Rushkoff submits that the government must encourage

> healthier forms of feedback through the very same media that are now transmitting such destructive behavioral codes. We can't counter the bottom-up terrorism bug with top-down public relations. We must spend less effort constructing false, politically motivated images of America, its leaders, and their intentions. These only feed the cognitive dissonance—the confusion—of those whose real experience tells them a very different story, making them more likely to imitate the violent forms of feedback they are already witnessing on the news or over the Internet.[45]

While it is highly debatable whether official strategic communication efforts promote "false" and "politically motivated" images, Rushkoff's underlying premise is sound: the government must use the same new media platforms and outlets that terrorist adversaries use to

---

[43] Douglas Rushkoff "Fighting the Terrorist Virus," *Discover Magazine*, December 4, 2006, http://discovermagazine.com/2006/dec/peer-review-terrorism-virus.

[44] Ibid.
[45] Ibid.

engage media prosumers in "honest conversation" about American policy and our intentions abroad. [46] Inherent in the idea of engagement is the notion of feedback. Engagement through dialogue depends on one's willingness and ability to effectively solicit, accept, and ultimately act upon prosumer feedback. Through the new media, we today have a much greater ability to harvest feedback than ever before; it is now simply an issue of will.

Strategic communicators can through the new media more effectively leverage emotion to engage prosumers.

The goal of strategic communication is not just to overtly influence how people think, but how they ultimately act. The most effective manner in which to elicit action from prosumers is through the design of dialogic communication that leverages emotion. Emotion is key to the process of action-taking. In traditional communication parlance, "the goal of making messages 'emotional' is to make people care. Feelings inspire people to act."[47]

The 2003 documentary *The Persuaders* delves into the world of behavioral marketing. In a nutshell, the film explores how brand marketers use an array of professionals in the hard sciences as well as the social sciences—from brain researchers to ethnographers—to design messages that nurture brand loyalty through the creation of durable emotional connections between specific audiences and the brand. Emotion foments brand loyalty by influencing thought and ultimately leads to a desired behavior or set of behaviors (remaining loyal to a brand when making purchases, encouraging friends and families to make similar purchases, etc.).[48]

---

[46] Ibid.
[47] Heath, Dan and Chip Heath. *Made to Stick: Why Some Ideas Survive and Others Die*. New York: Random House, 2007, 169.
[48] *Frontline*, "The Persuaders," PBS, November 9, 2003,
Http://www.pbs.org/wgbh/pages/frontline/shows/persuaders/

The importance of emotion in the marketing of brands, ideas, or messages is summed up by one prominent marketing figure in the documentary:

> You have to really dig into emotional connections with consumers. The rational side of life isn't enough. We've got too much information. We do not live in the information age anymore, nor do we live in the age of knowledge. We've gone hurtling past that. Once everybody has information and knowledge, it's no longer a competitive advantage. We live now in the age of the idea. What consumers want now is an emotional connection. They want to be able to connect with what's behind the brand, what's behind the promise. They're not going to buy simply rational. You feel the world through your senses, the five senses, and that's what's next.[49]

Dan and Chip Heath's excellent 2007 book, *Made to Stick*, offers a similar compelling argument for integrating emotion into messages. One of the key points presented in their discussion of emotion is that the difficulty in formulating messages that tap into audience emotion is knowing which emotion to tap. "The hard part," the authors note, "is finding the right emotion to harness."[50] Different messages are apt to tap into different emotions with different narrow audience segments; and different emotions will elicit very different thoughts, actions, or behaviors. The overarching idea is that in the contemporary segmented media environment, properly employed, emotion will be used to create highly tailored or customized messages designed for very narrow audience segments or groups.

The new media facilitate "nichecasting," making compartmentalized messages for specific audience segments much easier.

The new media make the practice of "nichecasting" or "narrowcasting" (as opposed to traditional "broadcasting") much easier. However, the new media reverse the traditional order of operations associated with message broadcasting. Instead of broadcasting a message addressing a specific situation or issue to a broad, faceless amalgam of audience members (many times

---

[49] Ibid.
[50] Dan Heath and Chip Heath, *Made to Stick*, 18.

through traditional mediators of news and information), the new media facilitate the identification of one or more specific audience segments *prior to* the construction of the message. Only when an appropriate niche audience has been identified does the process of designing a message tailored specifically for a niche audience begin. That is, a broadcast approach to strategic communication puts the cart before the horse, so to speak: the message ventures out into the media universe in search of an audience of media consumers who care. Leveraging the new media to "nichecast" allows strategic communicators to first locate a group that has identified itself as being concerned with a specific issue or issue set, and then engage this group in dialogue. One concrete example would be engaging members of the Facebook group focused on raising awareness of and support for Afghan refugees in Pakistan and Iran in order to highlight American efforts to assist the refugees and seek feedback and new ideas on how these efforts can be made more effective.

The most important point to glean from this discussion is that once a specific audience or group knows that you are conversing specifically with them and not broadcasting out messages with some vague hope that the message will reach nearly everyone in the media universe, the likelihood of a message spurring dialogue increases dramatically. And once you are engaged in authentic dialogue, your ability to inform and influence (and, in turn, be constructively informed and influenced) improves just as dramatically.

Those who execute policy/mission are the crucial missing link in new media strategic communication.

Strategic communication as envisioned by most government leaders is a responsibility delegated primarily to a cadre of professionals charged with disseminating official messages and information to the public. The pervading notion of who "does" strategic communication is responsible for the structure and composition of the Defense Department's Digital Engagement Team and the State Department's Digital Outreach Team. A group largely insulated from the formulation and/or execution of policy and planning is charged with communicating outwardly on behalf of the larger organization.

The self-synchronized cell and the re-framing of command and control discussed earlier is only one alternative for how strategic communication might be "done"—one that maintains the integrity of traditional concepts of professionalism and specialization. Control and task-level management of the work performed is delegated downward to group members, while command and operational oversight is retained at a higher level.

Another option exists. An alternative framework for communicating strategically—and one more suited to new media strategic communication—involves distributing the workflow among those individuals charged with executing policy and planning. That is, the practice of strategic communication would be performed in a distributed work environment; it would be the responsibility not of professional strategic communicators insulated from the policy execution process, but by those individuals directly charged with executing policy. The delegation of control in this context is conceived more properly as "delegation through distribution."

The case for "delegation through distribution" versus the formation of self-synchronized cells is two-fold. First, strategic communication performed by disparate small groups or individuals responsible for carrying out different aspects of policy injects humanness and transparency into the work being performed by, say, a Provincial Reconstruction Team. No longer is a faceless, distant institution—the Defense Department or the American government generically—seen as coordinating the construction of a new school in a specific province.

Instead, prosumers see and engage with a small team of in-country human beings sharing information and insight with a self-identified community of interest through the new media. In some contexts, this community of interest will be global in nature (a Facebook group formed around the issue of Afghan reconstruction, for example), while in other contexts this community of interest will be more localized (a mobile messaging group—which is essentially the SMS version of an e-mail distribution list—that allows interested locals to receive and/or send group messages about the progress of the school or provincial reconstruction in general).

Second, as already discussed, one of the chief advantages of leveraging the new media for strategic communication is the ability to solicit feedback. From the prosumer's perspective, the whole point of providing feedback is to tangibly influence or directly affect how policy or plans are executed. The work of the professional strategic communicator is typically wholly separate from the functions performed by individuals charged with implementing various facets of policy. Therefore, the feedback provided through the new media is not readily sent from prosumer to policy executor, but to a mediator or middleman that often will not be able to relay the feedback to the appropriate individual or group laterally (in an organization like the Defense Department, the individual charged with a specific function or responsible for plan execution may not be identifiable or reachable) or vertically (it may not be appropriate to send feedback to higher level officers in many situations).

Some effort has been made by those integrally involved in formulating (as opposed to just executing) policy to employ the new media for strategic communication purposes. Admiral Mullen's Twitter feed is but one example. While laudable for the example it has set, individual policy makers cannot reasonably seek feedback for the purpose of informing policy given the very limited amount of time they have to engage through a given new media outlet. Thousands of prosumers are following Admiral Mullen's Twitter feed, but are not able to provide feedback to his Twitter posts because Admiral Mullen is not following *their* feeds (how could he follow them all?). Thus, Admiral Mullen's Twitter feed is still operating under the auspices of the traditional influence model of communication whereby one-to-many message projection is the predominant form of communication occurring. Utilizing the new media in this manner is certainly acceptable, but leaders should not delude themselves into believing that the replication of one-to-many communication practices in the new media sphere is evidence that they or their respective organizations are adequately harnessing the power of the communication revolution unfolding.

Apart from audience segmentation, new media strategic communication accounts for technological segmentation or divergence.

Successful strategic communication is hard and only becoming more difficult. Advertisers and marketers have traditionally segmented audiences according to any number of distinguishing characteristics (age, race, gender, income level, physical location, etc.). Although strategic communicators have not typically sought (or needed) to segment audiences as faithfully as advertisers, official government communicators are, in a sense, marketers of information and are required to "microtarget" specific audience segments where and when appropriate.

Today, even more so than in the past, messages "marketed" by strategic communicators must compete with a wide array of other information streams reaching audiences not only through traditional media but through an expanding number of new media platforms. Thus, not only does the audience remain segmented, but the universe of communication platforms transmitting information is becoming ever more segmented. Therefore, as the new media become more prevalent more people are accessing information through more media outlets and platforms. And many audiences—especially Millennials—are accessing media outlets or using disparate platforms if not simultaneously, then in dizzying succession (e.g. listening to music and instant messaging on an iPod/iPhone and/or navigating online with active browser windows plugged into YouTube, Facebook, and one of any number of massively multiplayer online game environments).[51]

All of this has created a scenario whereby strategic communicators are operating in an environment in which the audience's dominant attention mode is one of "continuous partial attention."[52] This resultant competition for attention among diverse audience segments is one facet of what was over a decade ago dubbed the "Attention Economy."[53] In practical terms, a message's need to compete in the Attention Economy makes the job of contemporary strategic communicators much more complex than in decades past. Gone are the simple days of Edward Bernays—nephew of Sigmund Freud—who posited that a relatively small cadre of government and corporate influencers were able to exact almost absolute control over the public mind through the effective use and dissemination of "propaganda" through traditional media.[54]

New media strategic communication is multimodal.

---

[51] "A View from the Top: The State of the Digital Union," (panel lecture, Digital Media Conference, Silver Spring, MD, June 22, 2007).

[52] Linda Stone, "Attention: The Real Aphrodisiac," (lecture, O'Reilly Emerging Technology Conference, San Diego, CA, March 7, 2006).

[53] Michael H. Goldhaber, "Attention Shoppers," *Wired Magazine*, December 1997, http://www.wired.com/wired/archive/5.12/es_attention html.

[54] See Edward Bernays, *Propaganda* (New York: Horace Liveright Publishing, 1928). Note that Bernays associated "propaganda" with what he referred to as "public relations." The phrase "strategic communication" was not in use in Bernays' time, although his definition of public relations as it relates to government is close to what we today call strategic communication. Additionally, many of the activities described in the book fall more into the realm of what we call today psychological operations.

Many new media experts and communication theorists employ the term "convergence" to describe how new media platforms (e.g. mobile phone + iPod + GPS = iPhone) and, indeed, entire technology systems (e.g. Internet + telephony = Voice Over Internet Protocol, or VOIP) have coalesced in recent years to form new hybrid entities.[55] The idea embedded in this line of thinking is that following the proliferation of new media platforms there has been a welcome consolidation of devices and of systems that are re-introducing some semblance of order to the media universe. Future proliferative technological innovations, it is thought, will again be subject to the natural process of consolidation.

However, after careful consideration it becomes apparent that familiar media platforms have in no way been *replaced* or *subsumed* by "converged" media platforms. While the convergence of device functions and capabilities is clearly taking place, converged platforms and systems most often simply *compliment* existing ones.[56] Convergence has not led to the obsolescence of familiar media platforms (television sets and radios remain ubiquitous throughout the world, iPods remain popular, etc.), nor systems (obviously the fixed-line Internet and telephony are still with us). What this means is that it is increasingly difficult for strategic communicators to discern how best to select a platform through which to engage particular audience segments.

Media delivery choices have proliferated so much that organizations involved in strategic communication must exhibit the flexibility to exchange information through multiple modes. Being multimodal means maintaining the ability to initiate and sustain dialogue through multiple

---

[55] See Henry Jenkins, *Convergence Culture: Where Old and New Media Collide* (New York: NYU Press, 2006).
[56] Patrick Moorhead, "The Truth About Mobile & the Future of Personal Devices," (lecture, South By Southwest Interactive Conference, Austin, TX, March 13, 2007).

outlets (video sharing websites, social networking services, mobile social networking services, virtual world environments and MMOs, etc.) that are accessible via multiple platforms (mobile phones, Internet-connected computers, iPods/iPhones, etc.).

Al-Qa'ida's media wing, As-Sahab, for example, has been "multi-modal" for several years by:[57]

- making propaganda available through a wide array of new media outlets (video sharing websites like YouTube, file sharing websites like Rapidshare, embedded on social networking profile pages on, say, MySpace, as well as through traditional discussion forums and bulletin boards).

- offering subtitled video, dubbed video, and audio resources, as well as text transcripts of video and audio propaganda in Arabic, Urdu, Dari, English, French and other languages.

- disseminating sophisticated video products in wide screen format.

- distributing video and audio file formats playable on mobile devices.

- posting interactive jihadist video games available for download to engage younger audiences.

Not only does multi-modality serve to extend the reach of jihadist propaganda, it also gives rise to a system of communication with built-in redundancies that makes attempts to comprehensively thwart the digital exchange of jihadist material futile. If access to a favored file sharing service is blocked, any number of alternative file sharing services can be utilized, or the message can be proliferated on social video sharing websites like YouTube or LiveLeak, or

---

[57] See Media Tech blog 1 June 2007 and 17 Aug 2007 (GMP20070810208001) and 13 Feb 2007.

disseminated to mobile users via Multimedia Messaging Service (MMS, the multimedia equivalent of SMS).

New media strategic communication is persistent and pervasive.

Persistent and adaptive strategic communication efforts represent at a conceptual level a war without end, although it is a war waged in the information sphere. In the contemporary global media universe there is no termination criteria for strategic communication campaigns. In fact, there is no such thing as a new media strategic communication "campaign" since the new media conversation taking place among members of the "Always On" generation is persistent and without end. The narrative will evolve—even significantly—but the media conversation does not end. Eight years after Al-Qa'ida succeeded in projecting its message loud and clear to a global primetime audience, the organization's media operatives are still very much engaged in a never-ending strategic communication effort with a worldwide network of sympathic amateur prosumers who interpret, repurpose, and in some form or fashion proliferate the organization's messages.

In marketing terms, communicators "can't take a stop-start approach," according to one social networking executive. Communicators "must shift away from the campaign mindset. With campaigns, communicators "spend a lot of time, energy, and money trying to reach their audience. Three months pass by and then they're off to a new campaign." The persistence of the media conversation taking place is such that you are asking participants to "listen to your message or engage in conversation. You can't just dissappear after three months."[58]

---

[58] "Audience Engagement: Long Engagement," *New Media Age.* 11 October 2007, 23.

While government strategic communication efforts typically last longer than three months, the point is clear enough: the intent of new media strategic communication should be the design of messages meant to engage users through persistent dialogue. Antiquated methods based on successive "campaigns" with defined beginnings and ends are not applicable to strategic communication conducted in the new media sphere and may, in fact, even betray the fundamental nature of strategic communication as conceived of by luminaries such as Bernays, who long ago described the virtues of effective discourse as a "consistent, enduring effort to create or shape events to influence the relations of the public to an enterprise, idea, or group."[59] It is important to point out that one difficulty for military and civilian leaders is to develop persistent and congruent strategic communication efforts given the limited length of soldiers' tours and the impermanent nature of functional assignments.

Engagement through the new media must remain in permanent beta.

"If you're digital, then beta in its purest form will be a given," writes one forward-looking trend watching firm.[60] As mentioned previously, the new media are collapsing the strategic and operational communication spheres into a unitary communication space. The significance of this statement may not have been immediately apparent, and conceptually the two forms of communications will likely remain separate and distinct in doctrine for some time to come, although even Admiral Mullen has written that in taking "a harder look at strategic communication…the lines between strategic, operational, and tactical are blurred beyond distinction."[61] The final section of this paper delves into a more detailed explanation of how the

---

[59] Bernays, 25.

[60] "Foreverism: Consumers and Businesses Embracing Conversations, Lifestyles, and Products That are 'Never Done,'" Trendwatching.com, June/July 2009, 7.

[61] Michael Mullen. "Strategic Communication: Getting Back to Basics," Joint Forces Quarterly, issue 55, 4th Quarter 2009, 1.

convergence of time and space will render distinctions between operational and strategic communication largely irrelevant in the future communications environment. The intent of this final section is to illustrate that as the new media universe continues to march forward and evolve, any revamping of the government's current (strategic) communication effort will need to be updated and modified as Web 2.0 gives way to Web 3.0 and beyond. It should be underscored that the complex system of modern communication contains diverse interactive actors and artifacts that do not allow a definitive end state for how (strategic) communication is to be conducted.

As the Executive Director of Harvard University's trailblazing Global Voices initiative has written, "predictions about the shape of future media should be approached with caution. Few of the changes that occurred in social and participatory media in the past 10 years were foreseen. In three years, the discussion may be about entirely new tools and networks."[62] With this in mind, the section that follows offers but a broad overview of the new media universe's progression in the coming years. Some of the illustrative details may prove incorrect, but the general notion of what's to come is relatively clear to new media experts.

Web 3.0 and Beyond

As illustrated previously in Figure 1, Web 3.0 is conceptually tethered to the notion of immersion. Information technologies with ever increasing processing speed (think of Intel's 80-core teraflop microprocessor capable of 1 trillion calculations per second as a step toward the future), vastly improved mobile computing capacity, and proliferating media content and communication outlets are collectively leading us to a culmination point after which the rate of

---

[62] Ivan Sigal. "Digital Media in Conflict-Prone Societies," Center for International Media Assistance. 19 October, 2009, 21.

information flow will collapse many of the practical divisions separating strategic and operational communication. Both forms of communication will occur in real time across the same communication platforms and/or through the same information outlets. This is not to say that *cognitive* barriers will dissolve—some forms of communication will clearly still serve only to influence rather than mobilize or coordinate action—but the distinction between the two forms of communication will reside only in the mind of the prosumer and will no longer be a function of the technology employed to exchange information.

To flesh this idea out further, one must be familiar with the notion of *ubiquitous computing*. Alternatively known as pervasive computing, researchers at universities and venerable institutions such as the Palo Alto Research Center have been conceptualizing, developing, and refining ubiquitous computing technologies since the 1980s, and technology companies and other firms have successfully monetized some of these research initiatives.

Ubiquitous computing can be described as networks of sensors and processors embedded in the objects and surfaces of our everyday life that collect and communicate information to humans and other objects. More simply, ubiquitous computing is about putting chips into objects (walls, clothing, telephones, cereal boxes, lamp posts, stop lights, key chains, doorknobs, bathtubs, sewers, toasters, and just about anything else you can think of) and networking these objects together. Ubiquitous computing entails "processing power so distributed throughout the environment," writes one scholar, "that computers per se effectively disappear."[63] There is a close correlation between the "disappearance" of computers in computing theory and some of the theoretical conceptualizations related to net-centric warfare, such as "abstract machines" that taken together can be conceived of as "mechanism independent" communication networks

---

[63] Adam Greenfield, *Everyware: The Dawning Age of Ubiquitous Computing* (Berkeley, CA: New Riders, 2006), 1.

"thought of independently of their physical embodiments."[64] Those familiar with net-centric operations may recognize some commonalities with ubiquitous computing, although ubiquitous computing as a discipline is much broader than net-centric warfare.

One rudimentary form of ubiquitous computing with which many readers will be familiar is Near Field Communication (NFC), which allows inanimate objects to, in essence, talk to one another at close distances. The most common form of NFC is Radio Frequency Identification (RFID), the technology used in toll road payment systems (e.g. EZ Pass) and the new American passports. RFID chips are basically small transponders that can be embedded in or attached to almost any object (cars, phones, luggage tags, telephone poles, stickers, even human skin) to remotely (that is, virtually) provide locative, contextual, and identifying information about objects or even human beings. Mobile phones in use today with RFID readers (readers extract information out of objects) serve as an enabling technology whereby even the most mundane and inanimate objects may be equipped to "communicate."

Another example is that of Semacodes and the nearly identical Quick Response (QR) codes used in East Asia. These two-dimensional machine-readable barcodes are used as tags to "link physical objects to the universe of information on the Web."[65] Semacodes can be read by any Web-enabled camera phone with software downloaded free of charge from the Web. When prosumers snap a picture of the Semacode with their camera phone, the bar code is converted to a URL where information can be exchanged about an object, an object's location, or a planned event where an object is located. Semacodes are used, in essence, to annotate the physical world with information residing in the virtual world. Many researchers and developers involved in the

---

[64] Bousquet, Antoine. *The Scientific Way of Warfare: Order and Chaos on the Battlefields of Modernity,*" New York: Columbia University Press, 2009, 20.
[65] Chris Ulbrich, "Camera Phones Link World to Web," *Wired*, 18 May 2004.

development of Web 3.0 term the temporal-spatial aspect of the intermingling of the real and virtual worlds as the metaverse (a portmanteau of "meta," meaning beyond, and "universe").[66]

Examples of ubiquitous computing technologies reliant on GPS, TV GPS, WiFi, Bluetooth, WiMax/WiBro and other communication standards are too abundant to enumerate here. However, the key idea to be gleaned is that information streams will in the future be ubiquitous, in a much more literal sense than what we see today. Objects will communicate messages at the time an event occurs, frequently without the need for humans to activate or stimulate the information streams. As one expert submits, "Computing everywhere implies information everywhere."[67] All objects can be digitized through ubiquitous computing technologies. It thus follows that, "Everything digital can by its very nature be yoked together, and will be."[68]

Once nearly everything in the physical environment is networked (or easily able to be added to a network), prosumers will be *in* the Internet more so than today, although manifestations of the ubiquitous computing revolution are already apparent.[69] Being *in* the Internet will engender a reality very different from that which we currently experience. The "information-drenched physical environment"[70] of Web 3.0 and beyond is incrementally leading to what has variously been termed "augmented reality" or "mixed reality," defined as "the merging of real and virtual worlds to produce a new environment where physical and digital

---

[66] For a much richer definition and explanation of the metaverse, see the *Metaverse Roadmap Overview* available at http://metaverseroadmap.org/.

[67] Greenfield, *Everyware*, 23.

[68] Ibid, 97.

[69] See one example of communicative objects (Nike shoes and Apple iPods) at http://www.apple.com/ipod/nike/. For the theoretical underpinnings of objects that communicate *in* the Internet, see Julian Bleecker's *A Manifesto for Networked Objects — Cohabiting with Pigeons, Arphids and Aibos in the Internet of Things.* Available at: http://research.techkwondo.com/files/WhyThingsMatter.pdf.

[70] "Glossary," *Metaverse Roadmap Overview*, available at http://metaverseroadmap.org/inputs4.html#glossary

objects can co-exist and interact."[71] In laymen's terms, augmented reality is the process of infusing Internet-based virtual reality into nearly every facet and function of our lives (the real world as humans currently experience it), culminating at a point whereby two separate and distinct realities become indistinguishable and "augmented reality" simply becomes "reality." Augmented reality is the state of reality (human experience) associated with the metaverse (as a unique concept of space-time) referenced above. The Web 3.0 communication technologies discussed in this section are the embodiment of the experiential media illustrated in Graphic 1 of this paper.

It will not be possible for communicators to be anywhere other than *in* the Internet, interacting in real time with targeted prosumer communities of interest. No effect may be rendered by a communicator residing off the grid. But because information streams will carry messages at the time events occur, any communicator intending to persuade, influence, inform or otherwise affect a situation must be embedded in the applicable operational communication environment. That is, the strategic communicator of today who formulates outgoing messages, vets messages with peers or superiors, monitors and evaluates incoming information flows, etc. while insulated from operational or in-theater activities will be altogether obsolete in the metaverse. Tomorrow's strategic communicator will himself/herself serve as a prosumer in the metaverse; someone who produces, consumes, scrutinizes, navigates, mediates, and participates in the media-informational conversation among and between humans and objects *in* the Internet. The communicator will do so with an immediacy and persistence that is admittedly difficult for most of us to conceptualize from our current vantage point.

---

[71] Rashid, Omer, Will Bamford, Paul Coulton, Reuben Edwards, and Jurgen Scheible, "PAC-LAN: Mixed Reality Gaming with RFID-Enabled Mobile Phones," *Association of Computing Machinery Computer in Entertainment*, vol. 4, number 4, October 2006. p. 1.

Conclusion

To meet the exigencies of the complex communication environment of Web 3.0 and beyond, there can be no distinction between actor and communicator and no separation between functions. In other words, those doing the communicating must be the same persons acting in a given operational environment. In a very real contemporary context, the process of changing how strategic communication is done can be catalyzed by encouraging, even requiring, individual members of Provincial Reconstruction Teams (PRT) and District Support Teams (DST) in theater to engage and converse with other prosumers through an array of new media outlets, particularly those popular with specific prosumer segments (young Iraqi males, Afghan mobile users, etc.). Obviously, not all members of a PRT or DST will be capable of engagement in a foreign language, but even engagement through English-language new media on a much wider scale by military and government personnel will inject transparency into American reconstruction efforts and go a long way in fostering support in allied countries and raising morale at home.

None of this is to suggest that military and government leaders and communication professionals have no role to play in the contemporary or future strategic communication environment. To reiterate, strategic communication through traditional media will remain important well into the future and is most appropriately conducted through a cadre of communication professionals. However, the intent of this paper has been to re-conceptualize the breadth and scope of how we conceive of and define strategic communication by understanding the new media and how it is evolving. *The imperative we face is to adapt to the changing media universe by pursuing a course of action that utilizes the skills and abilities of nearly all military and government personnel in order to compete and succeed in the communication environment of today and prepare for the one of tomorrow.*

Indeed, broad guidelines to ensure operational security must be established—and continually refined and updated— before any step to delegate strategic communication responsibilities more broadly is taken, but OPSEC no longer justifies inaction. Either America's strategic communication efforts advance or our participation in the media conversation will dissipate until one day we face total obsolescence in the metaverse of Web 3.0 and beyond.

Bibliography

"A View from the Top: The State of the Digital Union." Panel lecture, Digital Media Conference, Silver Spring, MD, June 22, 2007.

Akkad, Omar el-. "Terror Goes Digital." *The Globe and Mail*, 3 April 2009.

Alberts, David and Richard Hayes. *Power to the Edge: Command and Control in the Information Age*, Washington, DC: CCRP Publications, 2003.

Arquilla, John, David Ronfeldt, Graham Fuller, and Melissa Fuller. *The Zapatista Social Netwar in Mexico*, Washington, DC: RAND Publishing, 1998.

Naji, Abu Bakr. *The Management of Savagery: The Most Critical Stage through Which the Umma Will Pass*. Translated by William McCants. Cambridge, MA: Harvard University Olin Institute for Strategic Studies, 2006.

Barabási, Albert-Lászlo. *Linked*. New York: Penguin Group, 2003.

Bar-Yam, Yaneer. *Making Things Work: Solving Complex Problems in a Complex World*. Brookline, MA: Knowledge Press, 2004.

Bernays, Edward. *Propaganda*, New York: Horace Liveright Publishing, 1928.

Bleecker, Julian. "A Manifesto for Networked Objects—Cohabiting with Pigeons, Arphids and Aibos in the Internet of Things." University of Southern California. http://research.techkwondo.com/files/WhyThingsMatter.pdf (accessed October 15, 2009).

Bousquet, Antoine. *The Scientific Way of Warfare: Order and Chaos on the Battlefields of Modernity*. New York: Columbia University Press, 2009.

Burton, Sandra. "People Power Redux." *Time Asia*, January 29, 2001.

Caldwell, William, Dennis Murphy, and Anton Menning. "Learning to Leverage New Media," *Military Review*, May-June 2009.

Cebrowski, Arthur K. and John J. Garstka. "Network-Centric Warfare: Its Origins and Future," *U.S. Naval Institute Proceedings Magazine*, January 1998.

Corman, Steven R., Angela Tretheway, and H.L. Goodall Jr., eds. *Weapons of Mass Persuasion: Strategic Communication to Combat Violent Extremism*. New York: Peter Lang Publishing, 2008.

Dartnell, Michael. *Insurgency Online*. Toronto: University of Toronto Press, 2006.

Feeney, Chekov, Vincent Browne, John Byrne and Colm Heatley. "Flames of Rage: How the Riots Happened and Why," *Village* (Ireland), March 2006.

Gharajedaghi, Jamshid. *Systems Thinking: Managing Chaos and Complexity*. Boston: Elsevier Publishing, 2006.

Goldhaber, Michael H. "Attention Shoppers." *Wired Magazine*, December 1997.

Greenfield, Adam. *Everyware: The Dawning Age of Ubiquitous Computing*. Berkeley, CA: New Riders, 2006.

Heath, Dan and Chip Heath. *Made to Stick*: *Why Some Ideas Survive and Others Die*. New York: Random House, 2007.

Jenkins, Henry. *Convergence Culture: Where Old and New Media Collide*. New York: NYU Press, 2006.

Lynch, Marc. "The Conversation," *The National* (Abu Dhabi, U.A.E.), February 29, 2009.

Matchette, Daniel. "Marketing as an Element of Strategic Communications." Civilian research project, United States Army War College, April 6, 2006.

"Metaverse Roadmap." Acceleration Studies Foundation. http://metaverseroadmap.org/resources.html#inputs (accessed October 15, 2009).

Moorhead, Patrick. "The Truth About Mobile & the Future of Personal Devices." Lecture, South By Southwest Interactive Conference, Austin, TX, March 13, 2007.

Mudgett, Carla. "Comprehensive U.S. Government Strategic Communication Policy: The Way Forward." MMAS Monograph, School of Advanced Military Studies, 2009.

Mullen, Michael. "Strategic Communication: Getting Back to Basics." *Joint Forces Quarterly*, no. 55 (4th Quarter 2009).

Perry, Robert, "Principles of Strategic Communication for a New Global Commons." Advanced Research Project, United States Naval War College, 2008.

Pintak, Lawrence and William A. Rugh. "A New Murrow for US Public Diplomacy." *The Daily Star* (Beirut, Lebanon), February 17, 2009.

Rashid, Omer, Will Bamford, Paul Coulton, Reuben Edwards, and Jurgen Scheible. "PAC-LAN: Mixed Reality Gaming with RFID-Enabled Mobile Phones." *Association of Computing Machinery Computer in Entertainment*, 4, no. 4, (October 2006).

Rheingold, Howard. *Smart Mobs: The Next Social Revolution*. New York: Perseus Books Group, 2002.

Rid, Thomas, and Marc Hecker. War *2.0: Irregular Warfare in the Information Age*. Westport, CT: Praeger International, 2009.

Robb, John. *Brave New War: The Next Stage of Terrorism and the End of Globalization*. Hoboken, NJ: John Wiley & Sons, 2007.

Rushkoff, Douglas. "Fighting the Terrorist Virus." *Discover Magazine*, December 4, 2006.

Senge, Peter. *The Fifth Discipline: The Art and Practice of the Learning Organization*. New York: Doubleday, 2006.

Shapiro, Andrew. *The Control Revolution.* New York: Perseus Books Group, 1999.

Sherkey, Mark B. "Strong Horses—Systems Thinking—Strategic Communication." MMAS Monograph, School of Advanced Military Studies, 2009.

Shirky, Clay. *Here Comes Everybody*. New York: Penguin Press, 2008.

Sigal, Ivan. *Digital Media in Conflict-Prone Societies*. Washington, DC: Center for International Media Assistance, 2009.

Stone, Linda. "Attention: The Real Aphrodisiac." Lecture, O'Reilly Emerging Technology Conference, San Diego, CA, March 7, 2006.

Thussu, Daya Kishan, and Des Freedman, eds. *War and the Media: Reporting Conflict 24/7*. London: SAGE Publications, 2003.

Ulbrich, Chris. "Camera Phones Link World to Web," *Wired Magazine*, May 18, 2004.

U.S. Department of Defense. *Joint Publication 3-0: Joint Operations*. Washington, D.C., February 13, 2008.

—. *Marine Corps Field Manual 1: Warfighting*. Washington, DC, 1989.

—. *Principles of Strategic Communication Guide*. Washington, D.C., August 15, 2008

—. Research and Engineering Rapid Reaction Technology Office. *Strategic Communication Science and Technology Plan*. Washington, D.C., April 2009.

U.S. National Security Council. Policy Coordinating Committee. *U.S. National Strategy for Public Diplomacy and Strategic Communication*. Washington D.C., June 2007.

U.S. Government Accountability Office. Report to Congressional Committees. *U.S. Public Diplomacy: Key Issues for Congressional Oversight.* GAO-09-679SP. Washington, D.C., May 2009.

—. Statement of International Affairs and Trade Director Jess T. Ford to U.S. House of Representatives Subcommittee on Science, the Departments of State, Justice, and Commerce, and Related Agencies. *State Department Efforts Lack Certain Communication Elements and Face Persistent Challenges.* GAO-06-707T. Washington, D.C., May 3, 2006.

Wasik, Bill. "My Crowd, Or, Phase 5: A Report From the Inventor of the Flash Mob." *Harper's Magazine*, March 2006.

Weinberger, David. *Everything is Miscellaneous*, New York: Times Books, 2007.

Wu, Susan. "Virtual Worlds and Virtual Humans: NPCs and Avatars." Panel presentation, South by Southwest Interactive Conference, Austin, TX, March 11, 2007.